Anchor in the Storm

Poems, Prayers, Stories, and Devotions

Vol. 1

2022 Conference Edition

Compiled by
Living Parables of Central Florida

Anchor in the Storm

Poems, Prayers, Stories, and Devotions

Vol. 1

2022 Conference Edition

Cover Illustration: Dave O'Connell
Cover Design: Bob Ousnamer

All interior images by istockphoto.com. Used by permission.

Published by EA Books Publishing a division of
Living Parables of Central Florida, Inc. a 501c3
EABooksPublishing.com

ACKNOWLEDGMENTS

We'd like to thank the directors of several Christian Writers' Conferences—Linda Gilden for the Carolina CWC, Kathy Bruins for The Well, and Lin Johnson for Write to Publish—for encouraging and equipping writers for the glory of the Kingdom of God. We wish to thank Cheri Cowell and her wonderful team at EABooks Publishing for giving us this opportunity. We thank our many friends and family for supporting us in our writing dreams. And most importantly, we want to thank our Lord and Savior Jesus Christ for His gifts—may this book bring you the honor and glory you deserve.

TABLE OF CONTENTS

INTRODUCTION

It is a daunting thing to submit your writing to a publisher. Doubts and fears prevent many from following their dream to become a published author. But these brave souls persevered. They overcame those doubts and fears, and they submitted. Then they waited. Those who've been chosen for inclusion have followed their dream, submitted to the process, and are now published authors. We are proud of them and are grateful you've joined them in celebrating this milestone. May you find encouragement in their writing to hold fast to the one Anchor that is trustworthy in every storm—Jesus!

Love Letters

Anna Moore Bradfield

Hey, Boo: I knew you before you knew yourself. I've loved you since I first heard your heartbeat. When I first saw you—my precious baby girl, all pink cheeks, lashes, and curls—I knew I'd found my kindred spirit. We were always communicating—no words needed. No need to explain myself with you; you had this rare sense of *knowing*. As you grew, our love deepened. We became inseparable.

So, what happened? How did we get here?

As I wait for dawn, questions swim in my head. Are you all right? Do you have a roof over your head? Are you safe? Do you understand the hurt your actions caused?

My heart aches, both for myself and for you. Are you scared? What are you planning? Do you think it's too late to turn back?

I've made my own mistakes along the way, but I always sought to do my best by you. The divorce turned your world upside down and turned me inside out. But we were there for each other, right?

I talked to your dad tonight. He's so upset about my catching you in bed with your boyfriend. He said he understands why I laid down extra rules but that it must've been hard on you. So hard that you moved out?

How could you choose this guy—a manipulative, conniving weasel—over the safety and security of home? Granted, you're 18. You can legally make that decision, but you haven't even graduated from high school.

Though I can't make you come back, I'll keep the door open and the light on, should you choose to return.

**

Mom: The night I left was the worst of my life. I wasn't trying to hurt you. I was trying to survive.

Do you see me? The real me—uncertain, broken, and scared?

Yeah, the divorce hurt. It hurt more watching you rebound from one guy to the next. When each relationship ended, I was there, just like when you and Dad broke up.

I always felt like I was second. I knew I was good enough to help pick up the pieces, but why couldn't I be good enough, period?

Those rules you laid down were too much. The only fair thing for me to do was leave.

The guy you see as a conniving weasel? I think he's cute, charming even. Everybody knows him. Everybody likes him. And he likes *me*. He makes me feel special.

**

Boo: So, your boss came to see me today. Seems you called into work—you know, that same place that I work? He told me you said, "My mom kicked me out. I need the night off to find someplace to live." You know that's not true. You chose to leave, all on your own. How could you do that? Say that? If you aimed to wound me, you succeeded.

If you aimed to kill my love, you failed. I won't stop loving you or wanting the best for you. I won't stop being honest with you. I won't stop being your mother.

You don't fool me. You're not so tough. You're hurting. Every wrong decision makes your psyche more fragile. Your reality seems warped. You seem out of control.

I pray the Lord uses whatever means necessary to drive you to your knees. It's time for you to get honest about your decisions. They may cost your health, maybe even your life.

I love you. Remember, a person is never stronger than when he or she admits weaknesses.

**

2

Mom: Yeah, I called in. Sorry if it embarrassed you. I didn't feel like I had a choice.

I know you love me, but you're hurting me, too. I'm not a kid. I don't need a daddy figure — some *Modern Family* cast that isn't real. Every time you start up with someone, you're turning your back on me to stand by a guy you barely know, who says and does things I don't trust.

I'm not grown either. I'm not ready for this world yet. Where do I go? Where do I belong? I need you, but I don't have you.

My guy — you know, "the weasel," — he has our life all planned. He says he loves me. He says I don't need to put up with you or your rules, and he's right. I pick him. Besides, you weren't going to pick me.

**

Boo: The last couple of weeks have taken their toll on you, haven't they? Are you eating okay? Are you eating at all?

We planned to have dinner last night. Remember? I looked forward to it all week. I came home at lunch to decorate the cake. I even left work early to prepare the meal, all your favorites. You didn't show. You didn't call.

When you finally bolted through the front door, just as I was turning in, you tracked in a cloud of chaos with you. You seemed pitiful. Feeble. Desperate. You flung accusations at me, demanding the title to your car — actually, my car.

As much as I want to pull you out of the mire and put you on the right path, I can't. Only you can do that. I hope and pray you do. Don't let one more hour lapse. Time is precious, and the road back gets longer by the minute. I love you always. I love you still. Don't ever forget how much.

**

Mom: I hate where we are right now, you and me. I hate that I came over, all demanding like that. It's not who I am, not who you raised me to be. It doesn't take away from how much I love you, from how much I miss you.

I think you and I are probably a little codependent. You've always been so self-assured and comfortable speaking your mind. That's hard for me. If I'm honest, I'll admit that I've taken on hurt — tiny little pieces of hurt, day after day, until I can't do it anymore. I've flung myself out of the nest, and it hurts so much! But maybe it'll correct what's so wrong about us.

I really do need the car and the title.

I love you.

**

Boo: I went to your school concert tonight — your senior show. I was anxious to see you, even if you wouldn't know I was there. You had to be there, right? Otherwise, you wouldn't pass the class. You weren't there.

Are you going to walk for graduation? Do you have enough credits? If I planned a graduation party, would you show?

I'd lay down my life for you, you know. I'd do anything to have you back, the way it used to be. I love you more than you'll ever know.

**

Mom: Sorry it's been so long since we talked. I've been out of state. I love you.

**

Boo: Out of state? What's going on?

**

Boo?

**

Boo: I turned 40 today. Happy birthday to me. I just knew I'd hear from you, until I didn't. I'm lonely without you. I don't feel whole. I want you in my life, but I can't force you. There's nothing you could do that would cause me to turn off my love.

Wait. That's it. I don't have control over anything you do—what you think, feel, or decide. I don't have control over your past or your future.

I have control over my love for you. That's all. There's nothing you can do that will separate me from my love for you. I'll love you and pray for you and celebrate you. I'll embrace you and the memories we've shared. I'll believe for you and for your future.

And I will see you. I do see you. I see you.

**

Mom: I'm here. I see you, too.

**

Hey, Boo: I've been so focused on being right that I lost track of how wrong I was in all this.

I took your love for granted. I figured you'd always be there.

The divorce should've been my warning that I can't control how other people respond to things. Yet, I'd convinced myself that the bond you and I share could weather any storm. When that bond was threatened, I blamed the conniving weas. . . . well, I blamed your guy for getting in the way. It wasn't him.

I wasn't ready to move on. The rebound attempts only distracted me from you, from us.

I'm sorry for the hurt I've caused you. I hope you forgive me.

Our love, precious as it is, isn't the anchor. Any love we might find in others won't be the anchor either. The only anchor that'll hold through this storm we call life is our relationship with Jesus. Jesus is the answer. He's our anchor.

**

Thanks, Momma. I needed to hear that. I'm sorry, too, for so much. I forgive you.

**

I forgive you, too, Boo. Love you.

**

Love you, too, Mom.

Anna Moore Bradfield has been spinning tales, exaggerating the truth, and flat-out lying almost as long as she could talk. Nowadays, she calls it fiction. She has contributed devotionals to *The Secret Place* and articles to *West Michigan Christian News* and the *Norton-Lakeshore Examiner*. Visit her website at www.AnnaMooreBradfield.com.

3, 2, 1, Breathe

Cathy B. Carden

She was beautiful but not defined by her tiny pale body. Steadily humming machines breathed for her as she lay in a coma, riddled with chemo and cancer. Dark, cloudy shadows jumped wildly outside the third-floor hospital window trying to snatch the last few seconds of this day. I loved this sweet girl beyond my heart and more profoundly than my soul, but I could not save her after our twenty-six months of battle. Today my dreaming child slipped away. At 5:16 p.m., the machines ground to a halt, their false breath of hope slowly whirring to silence. My six-year-old had been stolen in a dance between cancer and chemo.

The battle for her life was over. Left in its place was my own labored breathing of disbelief. I began preparing to vacate room 303 in ICU pediatrics. Often I dreamed about leaving this institution for the last time, but I never allowed myself to imagine this exit version. I surveyed our walls, then began silently untaping the sea of colorful prayers and encouraging pictures from strangers and friends. My cheeks stung with the excessive salt of grief pouring down them. This symbolic sea turned angry as I tried to decide whether I should try to save the messages, too, or throw them away. I distinctly remember trying to decide what to do, but I don't recall what I did.

The rest of that first year without her was just as foggy. Two months after she was gone, I managed to escape to the beach of Hopkins Belize for a few weeks to sort out just how mad I was at God, but the rest of the year's details are still impossible to remember.

Yes, I was angry at God. My child was gone, and I believed He'd ignored my prayers, or they hadn't been good enough somehow. I knew He knew I was mad because I told Him often, as I repeatedly ran and flopped into the Lion's Mane of Judah after yelling at the sea, where I thought He might hear me better.

He never retaliated, though. He's not at all like that. He's much more. What He knew intimately about me became the synopsis of why she came and why she left. Before her birth, I did not love anyone well, which is a harsh truth. When I wanted to love, I was afraid, so I often made it messy and always about me. Simultaneously I feared death and became a voracious fan of Ann Rice's Vampire Chronicles, longing to find the secret to forever by avoiding death altogether.

My tiny child solved both of those problems. I could not help but love her more than myself. Twenty-four hours before the end, she told me it was "ok" and meant it, having awakened from a dream where she laughed and smiled in her sleep. She knew and was kind enough to let me know, too. The next day she was gone.

From then on, I had one foot through heaven's gate, and I no longer feared death. I embraced it as the door to the very eternity I had longed for and had run from. Honestly, the God of the universe can refine anything.

Fourteen years since that destructive life quake, I was again sitting in the sand—this time with a more abundant grip on my story. This rainy, cold February Saturday, I had roped my five kids into another crazy idea. I dragged them to the lonely beach in the freezing rain by telling them it was a good idea, when it clearly wasn't. No one challenged me, but they scattered far and wide.

As I squinted through gray mist identifying who's who and who's paired up discussing how long we must stay or what's wrong with mom, I caught Marina far down the beach where the jetty met the ocean and sky. She was dancing wildly and singing a song to which only she knew the words. Her natural, Russian vibrato broke through the gales and space barrier, and I smiled. She had been loud even when she was very small.

I kept Marina and tacked on the middle name of Hope since she was Hope personified. Eleven years earlier, I had adopted her from a Ukrainian orphanage when she was five years old and when we all needed each other to stay alive. Her Down syndrome status meant she only had a long shot at being chosen by a family. The day I first saw her mischievous toddler face as I scrolled through a website of orphan photos, my heart split into a broken dam, gushing with determination to get her. I fought relentlessly as 18 months of paperwork and 6000 miles stood oppressively between us.

I peered through blowing hair and sand and took another deep breath. Unexpectedly, I am thankful for it all. The experience of rescuing Marina made up for the summer I lost. Memories of nervously flying to Ukraine with a pocketful of adoption cash, and instantly falling in love with pure sassy. I warmly embrace this rich memory flood.

Initially, I had applied for this child six days before her scheduled transfer to an asylum where she would have disappeared from life. She doesn't know that part of her story, but I do, and it haunts me as I look this beaten fact defiantly in the face.

What if I had never seen the beautiful little faces with the extra chromosome or scrolled past her photo on the internet? What if I had settled into my grief and lived a paralyzed life? Or what if Caylyn had not died the very moment she did? What if God had not added that extra cup of bravery to allow me to say yes to such an idea of international adoption?

These perfectly placed opportunities might have been dashed to nothingness, never to be; Hope lost. Did I trade one child for the other? Not even close. That was never my choice to make.

My position was to believe that God loves me endlessly, redeems broken hearts, and knows His plan. He can, He does, and He shines through gloriously every time. I seem to show up and mutter, "OK Lord," even though I sometimes do not feel like it. Some of His ideas look hard or feel painful. But in the end, His ideas won't be terrible. And in the very, very end I get to run into that happily ever that's always been in my heart.

Who but God understands the scales of life and death? The world has more questions than answers and collectively knows precious little about eternity. God elucidates life.

In Exodus 6 God told Moses His name, as written in Hebrew, was *YHWH*. We made it pronounceable by throwing in a couple of vowels, pronouncing it *Yahweh*. But take the vowels back out. Some people have pointed out that when we breathe, the sounds we make reflect this name of God. Breathe in, *YH*, breathe out *WH*. *YH, WH, YH, WH, YH, WH.*

Are we not continually calling His name? *YHWH* is our breath, and we never stop being connected to Him all the days of our lives. We are one breath away from eternity. The deeper the sigh, the closer He comes. YHWH has put His name as a fail-safe in each breath, so we are calling out to Him even when we feel like we are lost.

Cathy Carden is a word-gardener sowing tales of humor and truth. Rooted in Jesus, she fights for adoption, and those who have dealt with childhood trauma or have special needs. She loves family trips and keeps in touch with her first (not mom) name by singing seventies tunes and reflecting on when she was cool.

Run, Run as Fast as You Can

Gail Cartee

"Be sober, be vigilant; because your adversary the devil, as a roaring lion, walketh about, seeking whom he may devour."

1 Peter 5:6 (KJV)

The children dipped their hands in the cookie jar and pulled out gingerbread men. While they nibbled on the legs or bit off the heads, I read the story of *The Gingerbread Man* from one of many versions on my bookshelf.

The youngest children wanted me just to tell the story while they chimed in with "Run, run as fast as you can. Can't catch me I'm the gingerbread man."

You've probably enjoyed the same experience ending with giggles and cookie crumbs on the couch. But have you considered how much we are like gingerbread men?

In this story, a little old man and woman were childless so they decided to make a gingerbread boy. Different versions will tell different ways of creating the eyes and buttons and jacket, but at the very outset, the gingerbread boy was determined to run away. He even made fun of the little old man and the little old woman and all those who tried to get him to stop along the way. Where was he running to anyway?

Then the fox entered the scene. He didn't act like he wanted to eat the gingerbread boy. He seemed helpful. He was going to get the boy across the river that otherwise would have melted the cookie boy. The deeper the fox went into the water, the farther up on the fox the gingerbread boy had to climb to stay out of the water until — the gingerbread boy had to ride on the fox's nose. When all finally seemed safe, the fox flipped his snout, causing the cookie to go right in his mouth. End of story.

But is it?

Almost from the time we are born, we try to run away from our Creator and all those who would try to stop our running. Where are we going anyway? We laugh and make fun of those who try to warn us not to run to the world. Sadly, many allow that old sly fox to trick us into thinking the best life is the free life, the life to live as we please. Then, when the things of this world have taken their toll, we are left defeated, addicted, or worst of all — dead.

Let's evaluate where we are headed. Are we running in the wrong direction? Will we turn around like the Prodigal son in the story Jesus told in Luke 15 and return to our heavenly Father? He's waiting to receive us with open arms if we will only turn and run to Him.

Look again at the cookies. The gingerbread men are holding their arms wide open. They are not in running motion. Maybe they, too, are trying to tell us to open our arms and hearts to Jesus and run to Him.

Heavenly Father, we acknowledge that often we let the things of this world distract us from listening and following your best plan for our lives. Lord, help us evaluate our desires and turn back to you, running to you as fast as we can to your open and loving arms. In Jesus's name we pray, Amen.

Gail Cartee is a retired preschool teacher. Gail writes family devotions at her blog, gailcartee.blogspot.com. She is a regular contributor to Christian Children's Authors. She is a breakout facilitator for Write2Ignite, a conference for Christian writers of children's and young adult literature. She and her husband live in Upstate SC.

Jesus Is the Anchor

Michelle Davis

As the world was feeling the effects of COVID- 19, my own personal pandemic had begun.

A series of events would unfold and alter my life forever.

The rays of the summer sun were beating down and I could ignore the cries of my children no longer. "Mommy please, please can we splash today?" The thought of dipping my own toes in the cool water of my children's pool beneath the willow tree out front did sound enticing, but, he was out there, he always was.

Everyone has one, don't they? That neighbor who is always outside or lurking in their windows. "I'll take a Xanax, maybe two. He won't steal another day from my children." And with a swig from my beer I washed down the pills and gathered the troops.

My children ran circles around me as I lay the hose in the middle of the pool. We waited for the water to fill the blue pool. Their shouts and laughter made me smile, but my heart raced as I fought the sense of dread. My eyes darted back and forth as I tried to not look toward his house. "Were the cameras just moving?" I checked with my eldest to determine if he was there, watching us, or if my paranoia was so far gone I could no longer trust my own eyes. The garage door began to rise; my eyes had not failed me. My back straightened in anticipation of what foul-mouthed comments I might have to try to shelter my children from this day. But run and hide them inside, no, not today. I was not backing down. Maybe one more Xanax.

My descent into the abyss had not happened in a day. I didn't wake up and decide, "oh I know, I'm going to start drinking and popping pills today!"

The funny thing about sin is that it doesn't have to be abrupt. It can be that gentle tide that begins to creep in and before long has swept out where your feet can no longer touch the sand.

He stood just shy of our property line, casually talking to my children. Funny how adults can use their words with your children as weapons towards you. He was a master. Gone were the days I held my tongue and lifted prayers above in moments of crisis. The neighbor who hated me for being an immigrant, made my years of living next to him unbearable. I had become a prisoner in my own home. Today the tide had come in too deep for me to stand any longer and my feet were swept beneath me. In a moment of exasperation, I lost control of my temper despite the numerous Xanax or the alcohol I washed them down with. My hands reached into the cool water and one by one I launched bath toys in his direction.

I had tried medication, therapy, and even in journaling about my pain, but I had failed to surrender the pain that had come from leaving my homeland and gambling it all on life in a country where I knew only the man I had married. I had come to regret that gamble after the deaths of many loved ones back home shook me to my core. The life I had imagined we would have in America did not turn out as I had planned. I had stopped praying, stopped having fellowship with other believers, and stopped allowing Jesus to be on the throne of my life.

My actions that day had consequences. I had received my first criminal charge. Destruction of property. I awoke in the hospital suffering the effects of an overdose from the wicked cocktail of pills and booze. My husband stood beside me, describing the events that had transpired past my ability of recollection once the cocktail had taken full effect. I had no memory of the police or the ambulance, but the pain and shame across my husband's face was never more evident. He didn't know who I was any more, nor did I.

I had to pay restitution for my crime as part of a deal my lawyer had gotten me. My husband, fed up with me and my behavior insisted I would pay my debt alone and made me get a job and forgoing the ability to stay home and homeschool my children any longer. My once devoted heart to Jesus was swallowed by the typhoon of sin engulfed with hate and only a shell of my former self.

My Bibles remained on their shelves alongside my collection of Christian books. My bedtime routine of prayers and reading replaced with arguments, slamming of doors and bottles laying along my bedside. After paying my restitution I stayed employed. My children were no longer home during the day, and I found a false sense of value in my job. I was good at it, and the friendships I made with my co-workers replaced the friendships I had lost in leaving our church.

Little compromises here and there, those are ok, right? No big deal. The value I once found in the eyes of Jesus, and in the hearts of my children and husband was traded for promotions at work and paychecks.

The year 2020 blew in with a fury, knocking me to the ground with multiple surgeries, hospitalizations, and the finality of my moving from our marital home.

And then I had an accident at work, which ushered in a new level of low I didn't know was possible. The pain medication wasn't enough to keep me moving at a pace that I could sustain the workload I had taken on. The need for money had become my focus, but my injury which crushed my C4 and C5 while also damaging my cerebellum had forced me off work for months with no promised date to return. Drinking wasn't enough to treat the pain so when the once unthinkable option to turn to drugs opened its dark veil to me, I was swallowed nearly in an instant. I had never taken any drug before. But now I had become so far from who I was that I didn't care, either it would help me work the job I needed to survive, or it would kill me, I was ok with either answer.

The pandemic that hit my life reached far beyond that of COVID-19. I had turned to every anchor I could think of to keep me from being washed away. They all failed.

While I had a very narrow lens of the events that transpired, God was very much in control. While I felt the rise of the waves were so large they were going to swallow me whole at any moment, the truth of the matter was that I was still in His hands. God was moving through the waters, and I was still in his hands despite the beating I felt against me.

November 18th, 2021, was my last drink, my last drug. I had given my heart to God when I was 14 years old. I was a very broken child in desperate need of a father, so embracing God as my father was something I did with arms wide open. I knew how broken I was, with multiple mental and emotional diagnoses. I had lived for so many years with God my Father, Jesus my savior, but this year God was calling me to a new place in Him. He asked me, "Will you call me Lord?". I was astonished at this request. What an absurd question. To be honest, I was quite offended by His question, was He implying I was not saved? No dear friends, he was pointing me to an area of sin in my life that I had left wide open. I was ok with God being my Father, loving me like I so desperately wanted my earthly father to have loved me. I knew I was a screw-up and couldn't save myself, so it was easy to let Jesus do the saving. But Lord? This was a level I hadn't dared to let Him have before. The idea to trust that God's plans were good, despite what they may look like and feel like was more than I could have ever handled before. At 43, an addict/alcoholic, broken, and lost. I sat in the faith-based recovery center, letting Jesus be Lord for the first time in all my years. The waves have not stopped. But my perception of the storm has changed. I see now that Jesus is the only anchor that can keep me safe, and when the waves come, I have to just keep my eyes on Him, and I will not perish.

Michelle Davis is an emergent writer whose heart is to share with women that there is no pit deep enough, no sin strong enough that can separate one from the love of Jesus. When not writing Michelle is busy filling her days loving on her four children.

ANCHOR

Your Anchor Within

Audrey V. Hailstock

Whether young, or old

There's much to be said, yet much left untold

Of how to find refuge in the Savior's arms

From the tempestuous storms that come to do harm

But you can rest assured you'll be alright

Because your anchor within keeps you safe throughout the
darkest night

Like a flood, the enemy comes in to kill, steal, and destroy

To take away your peace, hope, love, and your God-given
joy

Though lightning is flashing, and the forecast is bleak

Foes are crashing, friends are dashing, and your support
system is weak

Pray and believe that depression, anxiety, fear, and doubt
are decreased

Because your anchor within is sure and your faith is
increased

Weather in air, at sea, or on land must heed God's sovereign demand

The wind and the waves become irenic; they must obey God's command

Whether within or without, don't wonder if storms will subside

For in times of trouble, God hides you in His pavilion and in peace you abide

When the hail of hurt beats upon your heart and you feel misunderstood and mistreated

Trust your anchor within to secure your victory; in Christ you're never defeated

The wickedness of this world worsens as Satan subtly tries to chart your course

Seeking whom he can devour and demolish with his demonic force

For victims of injustice, suicide, poverty, disease, and war we wail

Knowing that in the storms, the effectual fervent prayers of the righteous prevail

There remain many blessings in store as the LORD hears and answers your cries

Because your anchor within lets you see His Son shine and
the promise of clearer skies

Audrey Hailstock is an inspirational speaker whose passion is to help others overcome obstacles and reach their God-given goals. She's a graduate of Erskine College and a former teacher. She is married to Dr. James Hailstock, mother of Alex and Jessica, Spartanburg Ministers' Wives' president and Toastmasters Club 48 president.

"Jesus is the anchor for your soul. You get through the storm when the anchor holds you, not when you hold it."

—Stacey Hitch

Light in the Darkness

Larry Hoffeditz

Ever been spelunking? Each year I took my science classes into the dark shadows of a damp Missouri cave. Everyone wanted a working flashlight. But invariably, when deep into the cave, someone would want all the students to turn off their flashlights and experience utter darkness. It was so dark you could not see your hand right in front of your face. What a difference when the first light was lit after this. The pitch black darkness fled.

Lots of kids are afraid of the dark, even some of us older "kids." Being home alone at night is frightening. Without a nightlight, the boogeyman lurks under our beds. As a kid, I remember nights in the country by myself, with the closest neighbor well beyond screaming distance. Strange sounds would command my hairs to stand at attention.

Many times I have been at Christmas services where the lights were all turned out and candles were lit from one person to another. The darkness evaporated with the first flame. Brighter and brighter illumination appeared as the multitude glowed.

In an attempt to experience what blind friends live with, I have closed my eyes and maneuvered inside my home. Even with an awareness of where things were, I would bump into them, stub a toe, and get disoriented, not taking another step. Can you imagine a lifetime in darkness?

Likewise, ungodly "eyes" bring spiritual darkness. You've probably heard that our eyes are the gateway to our souls. "But if your eyes are unhealthy, your whole body will

23

be full of darkness. If then the light within you is darkness, how great is that darkness!" (Matthew 6:23).

And there's a dark message no one likes to hear, even in churches. It's about hell. Of course, I've heard a few good ole' boys let out some laughs while proclaiming they will have a great time partying with their buddies in hell. The reality is, hell awaits those who do not accept Christ as their Savior. Mark 9:48 warns that hell is, "where the worms that eat them do not die, and the fire is not quenched." I've seen worms die after being flooded out of their homes, but to never die in an "unquenchable fire," an unimaginable torment beyond scary!

Speaking of unbelievers, God's word further states, "They are wild waves of the sea, foaming up their shame; wandering stars, for whom blackest darkness has been reserved forever" (Jude 13, emphasis mine). The ESV version uses the phrase, "utter darkness." Can you imagine being stuck deep in an eternal cave without any light? And hearing others screaming "Help! Let me out!" along with you?

"This is the verdict: Light has come into the world, but people loved darkness instead of light because their deeds were evil. Everyone who does evil hates the light, and will not come into the light for fear that their deeds will be exposed" (John 3:19¬–20).

Speaking of darkness, *The Chicago Tribune* reported "Police statistics show most murders in the city happen from midnight to 4 a.m."[1]

If anyone knew of dark times, Job sure did. His ten sons and daughters died, along with all his servants, and over 10,000 animals. His wife told him to curse God and die. His

---

1   (https://www.chicagotribune.com/news/ct-xpm-2009-10-20-0910200159-story.html)

friends brought all kinds of accusations against him. And if that weren't enough, he was covered from head to toe with boils. Yet, after all this, Job said: "The LORD gave and the LORD has taken away; may the name of the LORD be praised" (Job 1:21). And again in Job 12:22, "He reveals the deep things of darkness and brings utter darkness into the light." As if in summary, Job 1:22 records, "In all this, Job did not sin by charging God with wrongdoing." Oh, to see the light as Job did!

There's a bright light in all this darkness. The Bible is full of light. As children of God, we are given a brilliant directing source of light: "Your word is a lamp for my feet, a light on my path" (Psalm 119:105).

Jesus laid claim to being the brightest light on earth in John 8:12. "I am the light of the world. Whoever follows me will never walk in darkness, but will have the light of life." John 1:4-5 announces, "In Him was life, and that life was the light of all mankind. The light shines in the darkness, and the darkness has not overcome it."

It's hard to imagine a place with no darkness. Hallelujah! Heaven will be a place filled with light. "There will be no more night. They will not need the light of a lamp or the light of the sun, for the Lord God will give them light. And they will reign for ever and ever" (Revelation 21:5).

Christians are called to be light to a darkened world. "You are the light of the world. A town built on a hill cannot be hidden. Neither do people light a lamp and put it under a bowl. Instead they put it on its stand, and it gives light to everyone in the house" (Matthew 5:14-15).

As a child in church, I sang "This Little Light of Mine." The words still flood my mind. Each verse ended with: "I'm going to let it shine, let it shine, let it shine, let it shine."

Hand motions for the song amplified its meaning:

First, a finger held up as a light, moving all around my neighborhood;

Next, one hand cupped over the finger as a bushel, and
quickly removing it shouting: "No, I'm gonna let it
shine!";
Then, declaring with a powerful blast, even Satan was
not going to blow it out;
Finally, pointing toward heaven promising I would let it
shine 'til Jesus comes.

A lasting memory of what our lives should be like
awaiting heaven.

The good news, the greatest news ever: Jesus suffered
death and dark separation from the Father on a cross, paying
for the sins of all mankind. "He is the atoning sacrifice for
our sins, and not only for ours but also for the sins of the
whole world" (1 John 2:2). By placing your trust in the Lord
Jesus Christ alone and accepting His complete payment for
all your sin, you are assured of an eternal home in heaven.
"Most assuredly, I say to you, he who believes in Me has
everlasting life" (John 6:47, NKJV). There is no longer fear of
eternal darkness separated from God. "For you were once
darkness, but now you are light in the Lord. Live as children
of light" (Ephesians 5:8).

Afraid of the deep cave of eternal darkness? I'm not, and
you don't have to be either. Let the Son shine in!

NOTE: All references are NIV unless otherwise noted.

Larry Hoffeditz taught science and Bible classes in Christian and public
high schools for 20 years. He currently teaches various Bible studies at
church and The Source, a homeless ministry. Larry and Joyce have been
married for seventeen years. They volunteer at CareNet, Safe Families,
and Missionary Flights. His degrees include Natural Science, Behavioral
Science, and Biblical Education.

My Anchor Holds Firm

Jacqueline D. Hooker

God has not promised us only sunshine and flowers. There will be rain, clouds, and storms. But He has promised to never leave us nor forsake us (Hebrews 13:5). He is always by our side and proves Himself faithful through it all.

My storms have come in the form of great loss. Loss of a brother, a husband, and a daughter. My brother was killed at the age of 8 by a drunk driver while walking along the road. My husband was killed in a head on collision with a drug-impaired driver. And my daughter passed away from complications of Lupus at the age of 12.

People who know my story often say, "You're a strong woman." Or, "Don't you feel like Job?"

Neither of these statements comfort me, even though I know they are meant to encourage. Instead, they lead me to trust in the only source of hope that I know, Jesus Christ. He has been my anchor in the midst of every storm and my calm in the center of what has seemed at times to try and overtake me. How am I able to still see Him amid the storms in my life? Because I know I can trust in His faithfulness. The hymn "Great is Thy Faithfulness" reminds me that He remains the same, no matter what. "There is no shadow of turning with Thee. Thou changest not, Thy compassions, they fail not, As thou hast been, Thou forever will be." This is His promise to us (Lamentations 3:22–23). His mercies are new every morning.

Married to my best friend, a stay-at-home mom to our 17-month-old daughter, and surrounded by a group of women who loved and cared for me. It was what I had always dreamed of. Melvin and I had met at Furman University in Greenville, SC in 1974 during my freshman year. He was a junior and the first African American Vice President of the Student body! I was impressed but not really attracted to him.

As the year progressed, I realized he was interested in me, and most of the students on campus thought we would make the perfect couple. We had our first date on the last night of my freshman year. I went home to Cross Anchor, SC for the summer, and he went to his summer job. When we arrived back at school in the fall, he convinced me to go out with him on double dates with his sister and her boyfriend.

I think I fell in love with him during that fall as I observed his compassion and concern for those in his circle. After Christmas break, we began to seriously date. He was a senior and much involved in student affairs on campus. He was the "man" when it came to politics and Black representation in all things on campus. He introduced new experiences and a world of possibilities to this smalltown girl. He graduated in 1976 and proposed that summer. We were married on December 18, 1976, halfway through my junior year. I graduated in 1978, and we moved to Nashville, Tennessee for Melvin's job. We were blessed with a daughter, Charslyn Olivia, on June 4, 1979. I was living my dream for sure!

In October of 1980, our family went to SC for a visit. On Saturday, October 25, we went to a movie and left Charslyn with my parents. As we left the house, something bit my shoulder. Being from the country, I didn't think much about it. As Melvin drove, however, I began to feel weakness in my feet, my legs, and then my arms. We stopped at the mall in Greenville to see if walking around would help. As we exited the car, I brushed a spider from my lap. As nothing seemed to help, we headed to the hospital. We took the spider with us. It was a black widow, and I was monitored to see if I needed the antidote.

After massive doses of muscle relaxers to ease the pain, I was sent home. I thought I was dying and, in my stupor, remember falling asleep on the back seat looking at Melvin and thinking how blessed I was to have him and what a great father he was to our daughter.

Suddenly I was jolted as I rolled off the back seat onto the floor. I called Melvin's name. All I heard was his deep sigh. Much after that is a blank, even to this day. A friend from my hometown came upon the accident. He says I gave him my parent's phone number, and he called for help.

As I was loaded into the ambulance, I asked about my husband. He was being transported in a separate ambulance. At the hospital, we learned my foot was broken. The bone was set and I waited for what seemed like hours before the minister who had married us came to the hospital to tell me that as a result of a head on collision, Melvin had passed away.

My first word was, "Why?" I was the goody-two-shoes girl. Tried to do all the right stuff. Went to the right school. Married the right man. Why would God allow this to happen to me? My whole life was about pleasing the people in my life—parents, husband, friends—and in the process, believing I was pleasing to the Lord. It was *not* supposed to be this way. I was a 24-year-old widow with a 17-month-old daughter. How was this God's plan for my life?

I went through the next year in a fog. I did all the right things. I took care of my daughter, worked a parttime job, paid the bills. God put so many ministering angels in my life through it all. From the business associates at the Southwestern Company in Nashville where Melvin had worked, their families, and to my church family, we didn't want for anything.

I was still seeking to know God's purpose and plan in this season. One day God reminded me of a ladies' Bible study I had attended a year before. I listened to the beautiful testimonies of these precious sisters talking about God's power working in their lives. He had healed them of disease, provided for financial needs, and worked miracles in their lives.

I had begun to pray, "Lord, I've never really experienced You in that way. Please give me a testimony."

So here I was. This was the answer to a prayer. God was using this circumstance to teach me that I desperately needed the Father to be my anchor in this storm. He showed Himself as a constant at every turn. He provided much love and care through both my family and Melvin's family. He provided financial blessings in ways I will never forget through the Southwestern Company. He provided spiritual and natural guidance through the women from my Bible study and others who helped me make wise financial decisions. I didn't understand "why?" but I did see His hands in everything. He had become my anchor in this storm.

"Storms don't last always," they say. But one thing for sure: In every storm our Anchor holds. In the power and might of Jesus, we can stand strong even amid the worst of storms. Sometimes it doesn't make sense. Sometimes it is fearful and heartbreaking. Then God reminds me of the joy that my husband brought to so many people. Eventually, I will see people in Heaven who will testify of how the Lord used Melvin to draw them to Christ.

I don't understand it all. But as my Grandma Carrie used to sing, "We'll understand it better by and by." I know that God will answer all my questions. It is enough to know that He is still my anchor in the storms of life. He has been faithful to provide in every way I could ever imagine. And, yes, "we have an anchor of the soul, both sure, and steadfast" (Hebrews 6:19). My anchor holds firm.

"Storms don't last always," they say. But storms will come and go. My confidence remains in Jesus Christ and His faithfulness.

TO BE CONTINUED…

Jacqueline Hooker, a graduate of Furman University, is a retired library children's specialist from Charlotte, NC. After 25 years inspiring children through storytelling and programs, she presently creates clothes for girls and their dolls. She is the mother of five daughters and the grandmother of six.

Anchors Aren't Just for Boats

Melody M Morrison

I'm fighting panic.

Breathe. Stay calm.

Find her.

A voice, *"But what if...?*

"Has anyone seen a little three-year-old girl in a red bathing
suit?"

She has very dark hair, brown eyes and she is so pretty.

She is so sweet.

Please, God, Please!

I carried the one-year-old on my left hip, with the five-year-
old holding my other hand.

I wasn't sure which direction to take

The last time I saw her she was squatting in the sand.

Just one minute ago.

She was just picking up shells.

I turned just long enough to change her little sister's wet
diaper.

To go home. Packing up to go home.

The waves are building

The wind is up.

Someone said the riptide is too strong today.

Oh, DEAR GOD.

What if someone took her?

Virginia Beach is so big.

"Lifeguard, do you see a little tiny girl

In a red polka dot bathing suit anywhere?

She's just three."

I am totally panicked now.

I can't let the other two go.

I have to find her. I can't go home.

If I lost her, I wouldn't want to go home.

It's starting to rain.

People are leaving. That's good.

No. That's horrid.

God. You see her! I know you do.

I don't. Please. I know you love her, too.

Let me find her.

You know where she is.

Please don't let the sea take her

Please don't let anyone else take her.

God, I am so sorry.

It's my fault. Help me.

I think I'm drowning.

I am on my knees weeping.

The tide is coming in.

The wind and rain are wild.

I search with my eyes,

Frantic.

Clinging to my other two.

Dear God. Please let her be all right.

Please let me find her.

⚓

"Ma'am, is this your little girl?"

Jessica runs to me. "Mommy, I found you!

"I was finding shells!

I looked up for you and you were gone."

The lady spoke, "She said she lost her mommy.

So, we just walked together

Back the way she came."

⚓

"I should tie an anchor to this one," I said.

"I think you already did.

She knew which way to go

To find you."

The lady touched my shoulder and walked away.

I wanted to say more.

I wanted to thank her again and again.

But she couldn't hear me call.

The storm was raging.

⚓

My blurry eyes caught the anchor pattern on the back of her
    bathing suit.

⚓

An anchor is not always heavy iron,

Shaped like a cross connected to a smile.

A raging storm does not have to be on the sea.

It can be in a mother's heart at the edge of the tide.

⚓

The anchor is what holds the boat in place.

God is my anchor. I knew he could see her.

Worse than a storm at sea is the turmoil

Of losing my child. Her anchor is me.

I must be stronger till

She builds her own boat

And her anchor is Him.

I am surely not enough alone.

Melody is a professional educator, mother, grandmother, musician,
speaker, writer and wife, not always in that order. Nothing means more
to her than bringing encouragement and Christ's vision of loving
children and adults through these roles. She and her husband love to
travel, research, read together, and wallow around in the joyful
adventure of wherever God puts them.

An Anchor In The Storm

Mr. Bruce

When winds are high,
waves crash the sky,
an anchor in the storm's
a must,
so ships aren't shattered,
swamped and sunk,
off rocks that make
their quest a bust.

The storms of life–
a metaphor–
we're terrified,
tossed up and down.
We wonder whether
we'll survive,
or battered, sink,
and, far worse, drown.

Our world today:
you have your way.
Write down life goals;
be bold in ink.
But when tsunamis
overwhelm,
some fear-filled souls
pick numbing drink.

Biz gurus claim,
"Stuff is the game.
Get all you can.
Can all you get."
They preach,
"The banker is the norm;
use other's funds
and you'll be set."

But should a war
drop oil supplies,
high finance crimes
cut off the cash,
their ship of fortune's
cast adrift,
elusive profits
In the trash.

So as you face
life's surging seas,
will bankers be
your go-to norm,
or choose the One
who walked on waves,
your Steadfast Anchor
in the storm?

Of all the gales
that round me rage,
this one is worst–
the storm within.
What hope have I,
my heart depraved,
my weary soul
so stained with sin?

O wretched man,
that's what I am,
I cannot do
the things I would.
The law of sin and death
attacks
the moment
I choose good.

When in the shade
of God, my Rock,
I'm sheltered, kept
in peace and calm.
My Anchor, Harbor,
Pilot, too.
I'm safe, secure
in Jesus' palm.

The Great Lakes State, his home,
he's earned the pen name Mr. Bruce:
he often gets accused,
"You sound so much like Dr. Seuss."
The Read-Aloud Dadvocate–
and yes,
he chose this title too.
His simple quest:
to teach all dads
the best thing
they can do..

Trusting My Shield of Faith

Norma R. Poore

"Lift up over all the [covering] shield of saving faith, upon which you can quench all the flaming missiles of the wicked [one]."
Ephesians 6:16 (Amplified)

The enemy lurked in the shadows brought on by the setting sun. Dark, beady eyes locked on his target. She turned the corner and headed toward him. The woman shuddered, looked around, and continued on her way.

Snickering, he rose, took aim, and released flaming arrows in rapid-fire succession. Target down. Success!

The victim? Me. The enemy in the shadows, Satan. I set my shield of faith aside because life was comfortable. Complacency made it easy to forget the battle and my real enemy, Satan.

I prayed, picked up my shield, and readied myself for battle.

The apostle Paul reminded believers in Ephesus — who were familiar with armor — of the reality of spiritual warfare and the need to stay on guard. But the only knowledge of armor I had was from movies — until I led a Bible study on the armor of God.

As I studied Ephesians 6 on PreceptAustin.org, I learned the word for shield meant door — not the round disc portrayed in the movies. Before a battle, soldiers took their door-sized, leather-bound, shields and drenched them with water to extinguish the fiery darts launched by the enemy.

A believer's shield is covered with water, too. The living water of Jesus, our Savior. The fiery missiles launched by the evil one are rendered ineffective when we stand firm behind our shields and trust Jesus to fight the battle, no matter how difficult or how long.

The army of Paul's time marched in tight formation. The men in the first row held their shields in front of them; the rest fell in line behind with shields over their heads. They marched shoulder to shoulder, shield to shield protecting each other from the enemy.

What a wonderful picture of how believers are to protect one another. We all experience hard times and need encouragement amid the flaming arrows hurled our way. I vividly remember when I experienced such a time and was in dire need of secure armor and prayer.

At that time, my youngest daughter had lived in different group homes for six years due to issues with her borderline personality disorder. My husband and I didn't have the training to help her. One day I was told her time at the group home had run out, per insurance. With no other options, she had to return home. My heart thudded. Fear engulfed me like a thick, wet blanket. If my daughter came back, then I would no longer be able to pursue activities such as writing, going out with friends, attending writing conferences, and leading Bible studies in my home. I'd have to provide 24/7 supervision.

"God, you're asking the impossible of me."

My options? Fall apart or retrieve my shield from the closet, stand firm, and wait on Him. I knew I couldn't stand without help, so I called on prayer warriors.

Like most moms, I want what's best for my children, but I also loved my lifestyle. I didn't want to give it up, especially for a situation that might bring daily upheaval and heartache to my entire family. The feeling of having no control and not knowing what to expect terrorized me. Another flaming arrow found a crack in my shield.

I cried. I prayed. I read my Bible. I repeated this process for hours.

Then my tears dried, while God's grace flooded my heart. The flames were extinguished, arrows removed, and fear subsided.

I surrendered all my dreams and plans to God, and repeated the words of Jesus, "Nevertheless, not my will, but yours be done."

My faith increased and once again I trusted Jesus, my shield, anchor, and fortress, to protect me from whatever lay ahead.

Tears came again. Not from fear, but joy because God met with me. He quenched the fiery arrows and brought peace.

Thirty minutes later, I received a call—my daughter was accepted into another program that met her needs. Hallelujah! I praised God for His provision. And since I know not every prayer is answered this way or this quickly, I was especially grateful.

A shield and an anchor are necessary elements of faith in Jesus Christ. One holds secure, while the other protects us from whatever is hurled our way during a storm. We don't actively fight; we simply surrender to God's plan, stand behind the shield, and allow Him to fight. He wins every time.

Is the enemy wearing you down with fear? Maybe, it's time to pull your shield from the closet, stand firm, and wait on God.

Father, help me remember to stand behind my shield of faith, firmly anchored to you, so I won't fall victim to the fiery darts hurled my way. Give me grace to surrender to your will, knowing you've already won the battle. In Jesus' name, amen.

Norma Poore, an award-winning writer, editing manager of Almost an Author, and co-host of Writers Chat. She's been married for 40 years, has six children, and eleven grandchildren. With transparency and hope from God's Word, she writes inspirational nonfiction for women. Connect with her at normapoore.com.

Goin' ta Jesus

Mary Anne Quinn

*Let the little children come to me, and do not hinder them, for the
kingdom of heaven belongs to such as these.*

Matthew 19:14 (NIV)

Bubbles. That's just what we need here, I concluded as I studied
my new, three-year-old friend. "My name's Alianna," she
declared with a pirouette, displaying the flair of both her
skirt and her personality. Definitely a bubbles kind of girl.

Her mom and grandfather had come to collect the
dining room set my husband and I were donating to a local
ministry. As I watched the grown-ups weaving around
Alianna, carrying chairs twice her size, I decided she needed
an out-of-the-way place that was safe and fun. I snagged two
bottles of bubbles from our front closet and led her outside.
We blew bubbles that danced with our laughter on a soft
breeze before popping on the grass, bushes, and each other.
Then I noticed one that just kept floating up.

"Look, Alianna," I exclaimed, "that bubble is going to
Jesus."

As Alianna tracked the rising bubble with widening
eyes, she made a joyful little bounce and rose up on her
tippy-toes as if she might just float up to heaven with it.
"Goin' ta Jesus!" she echoed, clapping her hands with
excitement.

At the same moment, a weight of guilt sent my heart
sinking. *Why did I just say that? That bubble isn't really going*

up to Jesus; we're going to see it pop any second. I've just set her up for disappointment.

It didn't pop. Together we watched the bubble continue to float up and out of our sight. *Jesus loves children, so He must love bubbles.* An image spontaneously formed in my mind of Jesus lounging on His throne, a bottle of bubbles in one hand and a pink plastic wand in the other. He was blowing bubbles, too, but His iridescent spheres morphed into hearts as they drifted gently down upon us.

Jesus' broad grin radiated His delight in joining our fun. I sensed him speak to my heart, "I like being with the kind of little girl who twirls when she tells you her name, and also the kind of woman who keeps bottles of bubbles in her closet. I'm that kind of God."

I knew Alianna's family had taught her that Jesus loves her, just as they cherish her themselves. With her buoyant personality, I could easily imagine her catching a ride on that bubble all the way to heaven and then running without hesitation right into Jesus' lap. I envied her carefree approach to life because I knew it came from the security of being protected, as well as loved, by the big people in her life.

Jesus' invitation to become like a child has often felt more threatening to me than appealing. I received love as a child, but there weren't any big people in my life who protected me, while there were many who violated my innocence. Being little meant being easy prey. I was once a girl who liked to twirl, too, but then I was forced to expose more than my smile and a pretty dress. Why would I ever want to be that vulnerable again? Now that I was an adult, a "big person" myself, all I wanted was to be safe. Yet, Jesus wanted to set me free.

Like the disciples who tried to shoo the little children away from Jesus, shame and fear had barred my heart from "goin' ta Jesus" with the same light-hearted spirit as Alianna. But the day Jesus showered me with bubbles and I bathed in His delight, I began a journey of learning to trust in a love that does no harm, discovering that affection need not be synonymous with violation. I still get scared at times, and I close off my heart again, but Jesus remains patient and gentle with me. It is safe to be small and vulnerable — with a great, big God to take care of me.

Now when I read or hear Jesus' words to "Let the little children come to me" (Matthew 19:14), I am free to run right into His arms. Just as I laughed and played with Alianna, I am also learning to laugh and have fun with Jesus. I am skipping forward with increasing child-like freedom — with one hand holding onto Jesus, the other holding a pink plastic wand.

Mary Anne lives in the Chicago area. She enjoys biking and birding in the local forest preserves, relaxing at the beach, and rooting for the Chicago Cubs. Her stories always focus on healing and building joy in the interactive presence of Jesus. Learn about her ministry and read more of her stories at www.creativelyattached.com.

This hope is a strong and trustworthy anchor for our souls. It leads us through the curtain into God's inner sanctuary.

Hebrews 6:19 (NLT)

Beach Glass: A Footprint of Hope

Linette Rainville

I'm gonna sit here Lord, until you give me SOMETHING I can hold on to, I shouted inside my head. I was desperate to hear God.

The whitecapped waves and glorious glow of the sun drew me in like a magnet that day. The clock on my car dash read: 8:07. "Good, I still have time to look for some beach glass before sunset." I grabbed my water bottle and looked around my car for a makeshift chair. I spotted my old quilted tote bag in the back seat. *This will do!*

I hurried to the beachfront, shaking off my sandals. Ahhh, the warm summer sand between my toes calmed my frazzled mind.

Spying out a quiet spot, I set down my shoes, bag, and water bottle. I began to walk the shore, making relaxing footprints in the sand. The cool lake water on my feet felt like an old friend. With every step, my eyes combed the shore for a treasured piece of beach glass.

"No luck. This time of day the beach is always picked over." I ambled back to my little spot on the sand.

The tide was beginning to go out, so I scooched my tote bag closer to shore, making myself a front row seat by the water's edge. I sat staring at the waves, feeling them roll across my toes, one right after the other.

I needed to hear God.

"Speak to me Lord, speak through these waves, speak through this sunset . . .

Here I am; where are you?"

Another wave swept over my bare feet.. I rolled up my Capri jeans a little higher as my thoughts drifted back to "the day." The events that occurred over the last few weeks tumbled over and over in my head, just like the rolling waves on the lake before me. I pulled out my cell phone and scrolled through his old text messages.

He wrote, "Are you home?" I had replied, "Be home soon, eta 5 min."

I was just finishing up a project at our Outreach Center, the ministry that my husband and I had established together. Dozens of thoughts had raced through my mind during the short commute home. He had be so very distant over the last few weeks... I could feel my heart pounding louder and louder the closer I got to our driveway.

Arriving just before my husband, I remember waiting anxiously at our kitchen table. The familiar sound of gravel under his tires alerted me to his arrival... HOME - to this same home we had dreamt of, saved for, built together and raised our family in.

Boom, boom, boom, my heart beat even harder. I was bracing myself to hear the reason why he had been avoiding me.

As I sat by the lake, my memory replayed everything in slow motion.

It all unfolded like a dramatic scene from a movie.

I sat waiting for him in our kitchen, and all I could hear was the blaring drumbeat of my heart, and oh yes, that annoying "buzz" from the kamikaze fly that flew in the door when my husband had walked in.

As an act of hope and faith for an intimate meal together, I had set the table earlier that day with two new paisley placemats and a mason jar of wildflowers.

He walked in, head down as he took the seat across from me at the same oak table, in the same beloved kitchen where we had made so many family memories.

He fiddled with the placemat, avoiding eye contact.

50

The minutes of awkward silence seemed to last for an eternity.

Speaking in a strange, matter-of-fact voice, he finally spoke out,

"I just don't love you anymore."

That pesky fly kept buzzing around the kitchen, almost distracting me from these inconceivable words coming from my husband of 30 years. That crazy fly sounded like a 747 jet plane as it continued to swarm around his head. He stood up, swatting at the fly, and then spoke the words I had already feared.

"I think it would be better if we just divorced, because there is no future for us."

He had made up his mind. He was officially informing me that he was walking away from our marriage, our ministry and our church.

"BREATH." I told myself.

A tight band gripped my chest.

I couldn't speak.

I was drowning in a flood of emotions.

I needed air.

I ran out of house and onto our front porch.

Finding solace in my favorite front porch rocker, I wept heaving sobs.

The kind of sobs toddlers make when they can't be comforted.

I couldn't catch my breath.

He walked onto the porch, standing a few feet away.

I could feel his uneasy presence.

He just stood there, staring at me, no expression, no explanation, no "I'm sorry," ...

no words.

"What? . . . How? . . . Do . . . you . . . love me . . . at all?"

I had barely been able to whisper these words as I wept.

So many questions swirled around my head like a hurricane.

How long have you felt this way?
Is there someone else?
Is there any hope?
No answer.

After what felt like an eternity, he had finally spoken.

"I'll be staying at a friend's cottage. I'll set up a time this week to pick up my things."

As my "husband" drove away, I watched the cloud of dust follow him down our dirt road.

There I stood—feeling alone, abandoned, and left behind.

Splash . . . giggle . . . splash!

The sounds of children laughing and playing brought me back to the lake shore . . . my healing place.

The cadence of the lake comforted me, as I watched each wave take its turn to rise, crash, and tumble onto the sunlit sand. How I wished these waves could roll away my heavy thoughts.

"Where are YOU GOD?

"Why can't I feel you? Especially now when I need you most?

"I feel like I'm in a thick fog. I try to read your word, but the letters keep getting jumbled on the page. I'm trying to listen, Lord... but I can't hear you."

"What is wrong with me?

O God! I need you! Speak to me.

Give me SOMETHING to hold on to!"

As the setting sun kissed the horizon, a majestic display of purple, red, and orange shimmered through streams of puffy white clouds. I took in a deep breath and closed my eyes.

Once again I listened to the comforting rhythm of the waves and cherished the warm summer breeze on my face.

My soul felt numb.

I rubbed my feet in the sand and dug down deeper until they reached the firm, cool, wet layer.

The rough sand made me feel a little bit more alive.

Each wave of the tide removed one layer of sand,

then another...

and another from the tops of my feet.

"This is the way I will heal. One layer at a time, one day at a time."

The next swoosh of water left a trail of bubbles over my feet.

Just then, a pale white piece of beach glass rolled right across my toes!

I picked it up before the next wave could wash it away.

Oh . . . my . . . goodness! I looked closely at the edges of the worn glass.

It was shaped just like a *FOOTPRINT*!

In that moment I could hear Jesus whisper to me,

"I see you daughter. I AM here . . . *it is now that I carry you."*

The Lord continued to clearly speak these words into my heart,

"I know that your life feels like a jagged piece of glass right now. So hurtfully broken, devalued, and discarded in the sea. But at just the right time, I will pluck you out of this "sea of adversity" and place you in a seat of honor... Trust me daughter, for I have you safely in the palm of my hand. I am turning your pain into purpose. I will use all your broken pieces...if you let me. Just like this "repurposed" beach glass, I intend to make something beautiful out of your brokenness."

The Lord met me on the beach that day. He answered my prayer and truly gave me a "treasure of hope" I could hold on to! My faith was anchored more and more in Him through that precious little footprint made of worn glass. My heart was once again filled with hope to believe that the painful, sharp and jagged edges of my life would someday become purposeful, smooth, and polished.

Many years have now passed since that little piece of sea glass found me. Can I just say… WOW…God is *faithful*! He has kept the promises He made on the shore that day.

Just like that broken, rejected piece of glass, my heart and my life have taken a new shape. I have found renewed purpose. My life and mission now helps others through their own storms- turning trials into triumphs through our Mentoring and Mission Builders Academy.

Friends, we serve a Mighty God who never wastes our pain. He has an amazing way of taking our "mess" and making it into our *message*.

My heart is overjoyed as I read these words of faith that I have personalized in the margin of my Bible:

"My ship was tossed to and fro, I cried out to the Lord and He reached out His hand to save me. He calmed the storm to a whisper and stilled the waves. He has brought me into His safe harbor!" (Psalm 107:29–30, NLT)

As a well-loved speaker, leader, coach and mentor, Linette carries a deep passion to see women healed and set free so they can discover, develop, and deploy God's purpose and calling on their lives. She is the Founder, CEO and visionary of Daughters United and Mission Builders Academy, a global mentoring and equipping ministry for women.

The Wind Blew and I Heard God

Jeanne Roberson

As I approached my property, I tried to absorb the scene. The roof of the carport laid crumbled on top of the two cars parked under it. The car that had been parked in front when we left was now behind the car that had been in the rear. They were both smashed. The washer and dryer had been tossed into the double-wide canal that bordered the back of our oceanfront home. The davits, which had once held our fishing boat, had become a mass of twisted debris.

The nauseating smell of rotting sea grass, mold, and damp wood filled the heavy, humid air. I could hear the familiar sound of the palms swaying softly in the warm ocean breeze. For a moment my mind drifted to happier days — watching tranquil sunrises, fishing, and swimming in the beautiful aqua blue water — only to be dismissed by the destruction surrounding me. I couldn't hold back the tears. As I stood amid the rubble, I realized we would never be able to live here again. Hurricane Georges had just blown through, leaving our world unrecognizable and forever changed.

I trudged through the devastation, trying to find something I could salvage. I found drawers without dressers, broken dishes, and furniture. Our clothing colored the landscape. The water had risen so high in the kitchen that it left a line halfway up the wall, where the refrigerator stood. My favorite pedestal cake dish was on the floor with seaweed clinging to the broken pieces of glass.

Much to my amazement, areas of our home appeared to be untouched. A shelf hanging on my three-year-old daughter's bedroom wall still had her little shoes perfectly lined up, as though nothing had ever happened. Yet, the adjacent wall had been completely torn down. My jewelry box was gone, and all my jewelry lost, except my wedding ring, watch, and diamond studs I wore the day we evacuated.

Drained, I decided to take one more look around the property. As I walked towards the canal, I saw something catching the sun's rays. I moved towards the swim ladder and bent to get a closer look. To my astonishment, intertwined with seaweed wrapped around the swim ladder was a gold chain my husband had given me for Christmas. It was rusted from the salt, but I knew it would come clean. I picked it up, held it to my chest, and sobbed.

Nearby, I found my AA medallion. It represented my sobriety and, I believe, God's way of saying, "Remember what's most important." Of all the things I could have found that day, nothing meant more to me than these two pieces. I knew I would get through this and my faith would sustain me.

I had not lived in this oceanfront home in the Florida Keys for very long. My husband and I were in the process of a divorce. We'd agreed that I'd take our two daughters and move to Florida to be with my mother, who was grieving the death of her companion.

In late August we'd loaded a truck and made the move. I enrolled my children in school, leased a storefront, ordered merchandise, and had begun the process of opening my shoe store, *Inspiring Soles*. I couldn't have imagined a devasting hurricane would soon uproot our lives even further.

Within days FEMA, the Red Cross and a multitude of insurance adjusters descended upon the Keys. We heard the buzz of chainsaws everywhere as residents began the daunting task of cleaning up. Eventually the water rescinded. Bulldozers came to remove mountains of debris discarded by the roadside.

Exhausted and overwhelmed, I struggled to get through those first few weeks while I waited on God. I never asked Him why this happened. I just prayed and trusted that He had a reason beyond my understanding. God gave me signs of His presence through people. I'm grateful I recognized those signs.

The Red Cross, FEMA, and neighboring business owners offered help and comforted. A church group showed up at my store. They prayed and encouraged me. I'll never forget the words someone from the group said: "If it was a good idea to open this store before the hurricane, then it's still a good idea."

They were right.

I secure a room in the hotel across the street from my store. The Red Cross helped us with clothing, toiletries, and food vouchers. I continued to pray. So many properties were damaged in the storm that it caused a housing shortage. The newspapers only came out twice a week, further frustrating people who were looking for a place to live, including myself.

All sense of normalcy eluded me. Not knowing what else to do, I walked across the street and opened my store, even though I didn't have merchandise.

Desperate to do something about my situation, I created a large housing board and hung it on the wall in my store. Owners who had properties repaired and ready to rent came and wrote their information on the board. Those who lost homes could come in and check the board during my regular business hours.

I placed a large donation box outside the entrance of *Inspiring Soles*. People donated new clothes, toys, diapers, and household goods. When the box was full, the Salvation

Army picked it up and distributed the items to needy families.

I met with someone from the board of realtors, hoping they would contact their seasonal property owners. If those owners would agree to make vacation homes available to rent at a reduced rate, this would alleviate some of the immediate need for housing. Most of those left homeless were year-round residents who worked in the service industry. These were the people who made the part-time residents' vacations enjoyable. Realtors worked hard, negotiating with owners, to get dozens of families into temporary homes.

I called local radio stations to ask them to help me spread information about the housing board. They were happy to help. The newspapers picked up the story too. Several articles were written about the housing board and my quest to help people. The stories led to a meeting with the local supervisor of the American Red Cross. At the meeting I became a Red Cross Volunteer, a position I still hold.

Through the housing board I found the perfect home for my own family, which was nestled on a bay, with a dock. We watched the sunrise in the morning and my daughters learned to fish.

Shipments began to arrive, and my business saw amazing success. I realized out of my own need, I helped hundreds of people, in turn helping myself.

The hurricane took my home, leaving me a changed human being. I found strength in myself I never knew I had. I found a deep compassion for others' situations and learned the importance of placing people over material things. My faith grew as I watched God give me back everything I lost and more.

I've learned circumstances are temporary, even when I can't see the light at the end of the tunnel. Whichever life disruption crosses our path, be it hurricane, tornado, or war,

God will provide in our darkest moments, sometimes in ways we can't see or anticipate. God put people in my life to encourage me. Strangers put their arms around me in my sorrow, and now they are dear friends. I learned that as hard as it was for me, others suffered more.

When you face challenges, put one foot in front of the other. Don't despair, don't ask why, just keep walking, one step at a time. Thank God for what you have, even if it's only the sunrise.

God has a plan for everyone. We may not know what His plan is while we're in the struggle, but in His time, it will be revealed. If we trust Him and remain faithful, He will provide in accordance with His will for us. In the storms of life, I learn some of my best lessons.

For years I've heard friends say "Jeanne, you are a survivor." I like to think I've done more than just survive. I've grown spiritually with every challenging situation God has allowed in my life.

"I can do all things through Christ who strengthens me" Philippians 4:13 NKJV has become my life verse, because I can! And you can too.

Jeanne Roberson is a Christian writer, speaker, and blogger. Her passion to inspire and encourage others to rise above the storms in life. through faith in God, is the driving force behind her message. Jeanne lives on the Treasure Coast in Florida with her husband their and little dog "Bengie."

Hope—the Anchor for your soul

By My Name, For My Name

Hannah Stevenson

"Sir, please leave," she shouted from the top of the building. "I'm going to jump, and I don't want you to see."

"Then go ahead. Jump," He held out His arms. "Jump, and I'll catch you."

She almost laughed. "No, no, thanks very much. Get out of the way."

He paused, "You don't trust Me?"

"What? No, it's not that."

"Then," he cracked a smile, "you don't believe Me?"

"No, it's not that I don't trust You, and it's not that I don't believe You. It's that I *know* if You tried to catch me jumping from this height, it'd kill us both."

"What makes you say that?"

"Experience."

"Experience with what?"

"You name it, and I've probably jumped into its arms. But I always end up bleeding and crushed on the concrete. It didn't take long until I learned there's no safety, no peace, no hope. So now," she spread her arms wide in a mock show of grandeur, "I jump to my death."

He frowned, "No safety, no peace, no hope. A sobering lesson."

Resigned, she spoke, "And one without exceptions."

"A hundred-thousand broken promises — that must hurt."

"More than You could ever know."

"You would be surprised what I know."

She heaved a deep breath, "What do you want from me, Sir?"

"You were made for promises. Did you know that?" She didn't respond, so He continued. "You were made for promises, made to be loved—made to jump and made to be caught. Your spirit knows this, and that, My child, is why you find yourself here over and over again. Those things you've jumped to in the past—those breathless gods—had no business promising you ease and unbroken pleasure, for even *I* refuse to promise you these things in this life."

In despair, she whispered, "Then what good are You?"

"I do not promise you immunity from suffering, but I do promise you peace and endurance in the midst of it and true life after it."

"You can't promise that."

"You don't yet know me, but I am not a man that I should lie, change, or become defiled. I am not money that I should run out. I am not acceptance that I should be revoked. I am not comfort that I would grow cold. I am not intoxication that I should only bury pain. I am not revelry that I should synthesize joy and then take it away in the morning."

"Then what are You? Who are You?"

"I am who I am, and I promise you—*by My name and for My name*—if you jump to Me, I will catch you."

And she did. And He did.

"For when God made a promise to Abraham, since He had no one greater by whom to swear, He swore by Himself... So when God desired to show more convincingly to the heirs of the promise the unchangeable character of His purpose, He guaranteed it with an oath, so that by two unchangeable things, in which it is impossible for God to lie, we who have fled for refuge might have strong encouragement to hold fast to the hope set before us. We have this as a sure and steadfast anchor of the soul . . . " (Hebrews 6:13, 17–19, ESV)

Hannah Stevenson's hobbies are feeling things, thinking about her feelings, telling Jesus about her thoughts, and writing what He says. She is at home wherever she finds dewy morning grass and is most likely to be found basking in sunshine like a lizard. Find her at: https://justanotherwillow.wordpress.com/

Navigating Our Ocean of Life

Anita Grace Williams

From the rugged cliff, blue-gray water sparkled in the sunshine. I held my breath as it oscillated, swelled and waned, and filled my vision. Closer to shore, waves crested, curled, and broke into whitewater rushing the beach with the sound of a chattering audience.

In the distance, where the sea kissed the sky, a U.S. Naval ship resembled a toy I could reach out and clutch. And although it seemed stationary, I watched it inch across the horizon, surging toward its destination.

Below my perch and way over to the right, I saw a marina. Docked schooners awaited their next big adventure, but some had already escaped. White sails caught the wind and puffed like heated marshmallows while their captains navigated the shifting water with graceful elegance. These stately vessels sliced the waves as easily as my spoon cuts blueberry gelatin.

Being a ten-year-old from the Midwest, I was in awe. This ocean scene fit everything I had ever imagined, but there was one more thing. In school, I learned oceans contained saltwater. And even though I'm from Ohio, where I knew only freshwater ponds and lakes, that day, I could have hailed from Missouri—The Show-Me State—I had to see for myself.

The coastline jutted in and out, creating inlets with beaches. And as I climbed down the pitted rocks, a fish-scented spray sprinkled my face making my descent slippery. The seagulls swooped and squawked overhead, but I finally reached the coarse sand of this Rhode Island beach and ran to the water.

An icy wave splashed against my body. I shivered and jumped back, but I was on a mission. Tiptoeing in, I tried not to think of scaly fish, slimy creatures, and the gross-looking seaweed now tangled about my legs. I just had to know. Was the ocean really salty? I took a deep breath, filled my cupped hands with ocean water, and took a sip.

"It's true!" I cried, throwing up my arms in a V. "The ocean is salty—just like the gargle Mom gives me for a sore throat!"

This experiment is one of my favorite memories, a memory I thought everyone should have, especially my six-year-old sister, who wasn't even born when I had my revelation. So, when we traveled back to Rhode Island — different beach, same ocean—I made sure she did research too.

At six, Amy was not as curious about ocean water as I was, yet I would not be stopped. I can't remember what I said to coerce her into tasting the ocean, but I remember her scream.

"Blah," she yelled, spitting. "Why did you make me do that?"

My mouth fell open. "I don't know," I said. "I tasted it. I thought you would want to see for yourself that ocean water is salty."

In my opinion, it was essential to know these things firsthand. But Amy taught me a big lesson. Not everyone likes to learn by experience.

Now, we're grown with adult children, and we've seen many changes, yet many things have stayed the same. The ocean remains salty, ships still appear as toys on the horizon, and from the beginning of time until this moment, puffy white sails move boats through the water.

These are comforting constants, and I've depended on them my entire life. But can I trust they'll always be there?

You might say yes, since our great God spread out the heavens, laid the foundation of the world, and said to Noah, "While the earth remains, seedtime and harvest, cold and heat, winter and summer, and day and night shall not cease."[1]

Still, notice God's first word in this Genesis passage—while—*ôwd* or *ôd* (pronounced ode) in Hebrew. It means *iteration* or *continuance*[2] and seems to indicate duration. As students of the Word, we understand the concept of the earth remaining for a particular period because other Scriptures agree. For instance, God, speaking through John, said our world, filled with lustful desire, is passing away. [3]

But when will the world pass away? And what signs characterize its end?

In Matthew's gospel, our loving Savior addressed similar questions just before He died for our sin, was buried, and arose the third day.[4] So, could Jesus have been speaking of the times in which we live when He said, "All these are the beginning of sorrows?"[5] Possibly.

Later, Paul wrote, "these...were written for our admonition, upon whom the ends of the ages have come.[6] If this final stage had come upon Paul and the people of his time, surely now, we are closer than ever.

Like it or not, perilous times[7] are here. The love of many grows cold. And lawlessness escalates with each passing day—paralleling a woman in labor—pain intensifying the closer to childbirth.[8]

Navigating our ocean of life has become treacherous—dark clouds of chaos and uncertainty about the future loom

---

[1] Genesis 8:22
[2] Strong's Exhausted Concordance—Hebrew #5750 pg. 103
[3] I John 2:17
[4] I Corinthians 15:3-4
[5] Matthew 24:8
[6] 1 Corinthians 10:11
[7] II Timothy 3:1-5
[8] Matthew 24:12; Isaiah 26:17

on our horizon, and the wind whips. The once peaceful, rolling swells of our ocean grow choppy and surge. Rogue waves crash down, drenching us with anxiety and fear. Our faces pale, and we can hardly catch our breath as we're tossed about on this threatening sea.

Dangerously close to capsizing, we frantically search for our anchor—our constants—the things we think we know, the unchangeables of our life, and our good memories of a simpler time. But hoisting this anchor, we realize it's too small and the line too short. "Is there another," we cry, "a larger anchor that will hold us fast and not let go?"

Out of our daunting turmoil comes a still, small voice. "I am the Lord," says Almighty God, "I do not change.[9] And even though the grass withers and the flower fades, My Word stands forever.[10] I am the True Constant. I rule the raging sea and rebuke the wind.[11] I alone search human hearts, understand every intent, and test the mind. My eyes run to and fro throughout the whole earth, to show Myself strong on behalf of those whose heart is loyal to Me.[12] Do you believe this? Do you believe in Me, and Jesus, God in flesh, who dwelt among you, died to pay your sin penalty, and lives forever to make intercession?[13]

"Do you understand what I have done for you—My gift of eternal life—salvation by My grace?[14] If you do, you are Mine. And even though you cannot see Me now, I am here. I will be with you in this turbulent ocean. I will never leave, and these waters will not overflow you.[15]

"Grab hold of your unseen hope—the faith I gave you[16] and never let go. Hope in God, dear one, for this Blessed

---

9 Malachi 3:6
10 Isaiah 40:8
11 Psalm 89:9; Mark 4:39
12 I Chronicles 28:9; Jeremiah 17:10; II Chronicles 16:9
13 Hebrews 7:25
14 Romans 6:23; Ephesians 2:8-10
15 Hebrews 13:5; Isaiah 43:1-3
16 Romans 8:24-25; Hebrews 11:1; Romans 12:3

Hope is your soul's strong, sure, and steadfast Anchor. [17]Cling to Me and fear not...I am your God. My grace is sufficient, and in your weakness, My power is perfected. I will strengthen you and help you. And, come what may, I will bring you through and set you safely upon the shore."[18]

PRAYER: Oh LORD my God, Anchor of my soul, thank You. Today, You have reassured me, increased my faith, and caused me to place all my trust in You as my only sin forgiver. While chaos and uncertainty strive to sink me, I know You are my Savior. In this world, troubles abound, but You have overcome the world. Your peace fills me, Your Spirit comforts, and I have joy in my journey.[19] In Jesus' name, amen.

Anita, a member of Alliance Friends Church, has studied and taught Bible studies and Sunday school for 35 years. For 15 years, Anita's written a monthly devotional newsletter and has blogged since 2012 (www.meatforthehungry.com). She's the former Programs and Devotional Editor/Writer for Women's Missionary Fellowship, Evangelical Friends Church — North America.

---

[17] Psalm 42:5; I Peter 1:21; Titus 2:13; Hebrews 6:19
[18] Isaiah 41:10; II Corinthians 12:9; Ezekiel 47:1-6
[19] John 16:33; John 14:26-27

Living Parables of Central Florida, Inc., of which EABooks Publishing is a division, supports Christian charities providing for the needs of their communities. Ministries are encouraged to join hands and hearts with like-minded charities to better meet unmet needs in their communities. Annually the Board of Directors chooses the recipients of seed money to facilitate the beginning stages of these charitable activities.

Mission Statement

To empower start up, nonprofit organizations financially, spiritually, and with sound business knowledge to participate successfully as a responsible 501(c)3 organization that contributes to the Kingdom work of God.

GPS Grant Program

The goal of the GPS Program: The GPS (God's Positioning System) provides a solid foundation for running a successful non-profit through a year-long coaching process and a grant for start-up needs, eventually allowing these charities to successfully apply for grants and loans from others so they can further meet unmet needs in their communities.

Made in the USA
Monee, IL
17 December 2022

22270957R00046